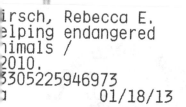

HELPING ENDANGERED ANIMALS

by Rebecca E. Hirsch

CHERRY LAKE PUBLISHING • ANN ARBOR, MICHIGAN

Published in the United States of America
by Cherry Lake Publishing
Ann Arbor, Michigan
www.cherrylakepublishing.com

Printed in the United States of America
Corporate Graphics Inc
January 2010
CLSP06

Consultants: Mark C. Andersen, professor of fish, wildlife and conservation ecology,
New Mexico State University; Gail Saunders-Smith, associate professor of literacy,
Beeghly College of Education, Youngstown State University

Editorial direction: Book design and illustration:
Melissa Johnson   Emily Love

Photo credits: Kitch Bain/Shutterstock Images, cover, 1; John Hofboer/Fotolia, 5; Kitch
Bain/Fotolia, 7; Fotolia, 11, 14, 18, 24, 27; NOAA National Marine Fisheries Service, 12;
Anders Tornberg/iStockphoto, 22

Library of Congress Cataloging-in-Publication Data
Hirsch, Rebecca E.
  Save the planet : helping endangered animals / by Rebecca Hirsch.
     p. cm. — (Language arts explorer)
  Includes index.
  ISBN 978-1-60279-658-4 (hardback) — ISBN 978-1-60279-667-6 (pbk.)
  1. Endangered species—Juvenile literature. I. Title. II. Series.

QL83.H57 2010
591.68—dc22

                              2009038094

**Cherry Lake Publishing would like to acknowledge the work of The Partnership for 21st
Century Skills. Please visit www.21centuryskills.org for more information.**

TABLE OF CONTENTS

Your Mission 4

What You Know 4

Qinling Mountains, China.............................6

Zakouma Park, Chad....................................9

Lubec, Maine 12

National Zoo..16

Churchill, Manitoba......................................20

Blackwater Wildlife Refuge 23

Mission Accomplished!.................................26

Consider This...26

Glossary 28

Learn More 29

Further Missions 30

Index 31

You are being given a mission. The facts in What You Know will help you accomplish it. Remember What You Know while you are reading the story. The story will help you answer the questions at the end of the book. Have fun on this adventure!

Your mission is to investigate animals in trouble. Many animals today are in danger. What does it mean when we say an animal is endangered? Why are animals threatened and what can people do to help them survive? Remember to keep What You Know in mind during your investigation.

★ Animals have adaptations that help them survive where they live. An adaptation might be the way an animal finds food or defends itself. An adaptation could be a change in its body like the shape of its feet or the color of its fur.

★ Extinction happens when all members of a species die. The animal is gone forever.

★ Humans and all living things are connected. When an animal becomes extinct, other living things around it are affected.

People try to help save animals, including elephants, from extinction.

We are going to take a field trip around the world to meet some animals that are in trouble. Join us on this exciting adventure!

We came to the Qinling Mountain region in China. Giant pandas used to live all over southern and eastern China and in a few neighboring countries. Now they live in just a few places here.

Pandas are endangered. That means there are so few remaining that they could soon become extinct. What has happened to the pandas?

Where Pandas Live

We went to see the places where giant pandas still live. We found a local guide to lead us. Pandas live in bamboo-filled forests high in the mountains. Our guide led us up a trail into the mountaintop forest. The air was foggy and damp. Bamboo grew everywhere. We saw no giant pandas, but we did see places where pandas had been. The pandas had eaten bamboo and left scratch marks on trees. The guide told us that pandas eat lots and lots of bamboo and almost nothing else.

After our hike, we walked into the valley. We met some farmers who were cutting down bamboo. The farmers told us they were clearing the land for farms. The people are poor. Farming gives them a way to earn a living. Loss of

Pandas need bamboo to eat.

habitat is a big problem for pandas. People continue to move higher up the mountain slopes. They cut down pandas' habitat. Without the bamboo forests, the pandas cannot survive.

THE VALUE OF THE BAMBOO FORESTS

Protecting mountain habitats not only helps pandas, but it also helps people and other wildlife. The mountains of China are home to other endangered animals such as the golden monkey and a bird called the crested ibis. In addition, millions of people drink from the rivers that flow through the forests. Preserving the forests helps keep the water clean.

Fragmented Habitat

Another problem is that the pandas' habitat is fragmented, or broken up in scattered patches. One patch of bamboo forest is not connected to another. Pandas need a way to get from one area of forest to another. They need a safe way to find food and other pandas.

The good news is that people all over the world are working to save pandas. The World Wildlife Fund (WWF) teaches local people how to use the land without hurting the pandas' habitat. For example, the Chinese government has created nature reserves and corridors filled with bamboo. The corridors connect isolated forests, giving some pandas safer ways to move from place to place. ★

Next we arrived in Zakouma National Park in the country of Chad in Africa. This reserve is home to the largest animal on land, the African elephant, as well as birds, lions, and other mammals.

We traveled through the park until we reached our base camp. The camp was beside a pool of water. Scientists and park rangers greeted us. The scientists are in the park to count elephants. The rangers patrol the park and keep wildlife safe.

A ranger explained that it is the dry season in this part of Africa. Water is scarce. Zakouma is one of the few places around that has water, making it a good place for animals to live.

Watching the Elephants

Just then a herd of about 30 elephants approached the watering hole. Everyone stopped talking and watched the elephant mothers with their babies. The mothers nudged their babies forward to the pool. The elephants lowered their trunks into the cool water and splashed themselves. The young elephants played in the water. The adults watched from the bank, flapping their giant ears to

HABITAT FOR AFRICAN ELEPHANTS

Many people in Africa don't have enough food to eat. They cut down or burn animal habitats to make room for farms. Habitat loss is a big problem for African elephants.

keep cool. Then the elephants left the watering hole and continued on their way.

The ranger said that not many elephants are left in Zakouma. Poachers have killed most of the elephants. The poachers kill adult elephants and take their tusks for ivory. Calves are safe from poachers because they don't have tusks. But a baby elephant without its mother is not safe from predators. Orphaned baby elephants are often killed by lions.

Killing elephants is illegal in Zakouma, but many people in this part of Africa are poor. Selling ivory is one way to make money. Rangers patrol the reserve, looking for poachers and working to keep elephants safe.

Difficult to Protect

If the rangers are protecting elephants, why are so many of the animals dying? The problem is that the elephants don't stay in the park. When the rains begin,

Poachers kill elephants for their tusks.

elephants leave Zakouma to find more food. Rangers can't help the elephants once the animals leave the reserve. Poachers sometimes sit outside the borders of the park, waiting for elephants.

Africa is a difficult place to protect endangered species. In many places people are hungry. Wars break out. The fighting puts animals and the people working to save them in danger. A country struggling with war and hunger is unlikely to have enough money to protect its animals. ★

We traveled to Lubec, Maine, on the Atlantic Ocean next. Whale researchers come to Lubec every year to observe right whales during the summer. One of the scientists told us the whales' story.

Hunted Whales

For hundreds of years, people hunted right whales. That is how the animals got their name. They were the "right whale" to hunt because they were slow and easy to catch, and they did not sink when they died. All this

People hunted right whales before the 1930s.

hunting harmed the whale population. Fewer and fewer right whales remained in the North Atlantic. At one time only about 100 North Atlantic right whales were left. People realized the whales could become extinct. So hunting right whales was banned in most countries in the 1930s.

The whale population recovered, but very slowly. The animals were still in danger of extinction. One problem was that people were killing them by accident. Some whales were hit by ships. Others died tangled in fishing lines or nets. Another problem is that right whales have a low birthrate. A female might give birth to only one calf every three years. People worried the whales were not having enough babies to keep the population growing.

SAVING WHALES FROM FISHING LINES

Whale researchers are still working on the problem of fishing lines. Many right whales become tangled in fishing gear and die. The sharp ropes cut through their skin or strangle them. Researchers are working on new fishing gear that may help keep whales safe.

The right whale population might be recovering.

Studying Whales

In the 1980s, scientists started studying the whales. They hoped to find a way to save the animals. So they studied where right whales gathered. They traveled into whale habitats and counted the whales. Much of this work was paid for by the U.S. government. It cost a lot of money.

Some people thought the effort was a waste. They thought the right whales should be given up as a lost cause.

But others continued to believe the right whales could be saved. If just a few whales could be saved each year, it might be enough to keep the population growing. Now that people knew where the whales gathered, they could try to keep ships out of the way.

Rules Protect Whales

In the 1990s, new rules were put into place for ships. Ship captains were warned when they were entering an area where whales were swimming. Some ships changed course to avoid whale habitats. Many ships slowed their speed in whale areas.

The changes made a difference. In 2008, for the first time since the 1600s, not a single North Atlantic right whale died at human hands. Then some more good news came. In just one year, 38 calves were born. That set a new record. Perhaps right whales would survive after all.

Right whales have taught people an important lesson: Sometimes simple changes can make a difference. It is too soon to know whether North Atlantic right whales can be saved. But they are doing better than they have for a long time. ★

We visited the National Zoo in Washington DC to learn about the golden lion tamarin. As we walked through the zoo, we could see these small monkeys climbing in trees overhead. The tamarin almost became extinct but now is recovering. We heard that zoos played a part. We were eager to learn more.

Breeding in Zoos

A zookeeper told us that golden lion tamarins live in the Atlantic rain forest along the coast of Brazil. Most of the Atlantic rain forest has been cut down. The little that remains is fragmented in small patches. Not long ago, the monkeys were on the verge of becoming extinct. At one point, only 200 golden lion tamarins were left.

THE ATLANTIC RAIN FOREST

The Atlantic rain forest in South America is home to 2,000 different butterflies and 20,000 kinds of plants. Nearly 950 different birds live here, many of which can be found nowhere else on Earth. Saving the rain forest helps these plants and animals that share the tamarins' home.

Conservationists realized that the only hope for the monkeys was to move them to zoos. Zookeepers would need to do more than just house the animals. They would need to breed them to keep the species going.

At first, the golden lion tamarins in zoos didn't produce any babies. Zoo workers were worried. They experimented. They tried giving the monkeys different foods. They moved the animals out of larger groups and into smaller, family-sized groups. Finally, the monkeys began to have babies. The population of tamarins in zoos grew.

Back to the Wild

After a while, there were enough tamarins in zoos that people wanted to reintroduce the monkeys into the wild. The first step was finding a place for the tamarins. The government of Brazil agreed to set aside a reserve, where the rain forest would be protected. But people were still cutting down trees in the reserve. Some local people were removing the few remaining wild tamarins to keep as pets. For tamarins to have a chance, local people would need to help.

Conservation workers began to teach people about the problems. They put messages about tamarins on television, books, and T-shirts. The message got out. Local people now wanted to save the tamarins and their rain-forest home.

Zookeepers bred golden lion tamarins
to help the species survive.

But there were other challenges. A big problem was that the zoo tamarins didn't behave like wild animals anymore. These tamarins had lived their whole lives in zoos. They didn't know how to survive in the rain forest. Zoo workers tried to teach the tamarins how to be wild. They hid the animals' meals so the tamarins would learn to find food. At the National Zoo, workers let the tamarins out of their cages so the animals could practice climbing trees.

Even so, when zoo-born tamarins were brought back to the jungle, many didn't do well. Some died soon after their release, but a few survived. They mated with the few wild tamarins left in the jungle and produced babies.

Hope for Recovery

The reintroduction program helped save golden lion tamarins from extinction. Today approximately 1,500 tamarins live in the rain forest. Many of them are the offspring of zoo-born tamarins. Other actions helped save the tamarins, too. More nature reserves were created. Isolated patches of rain forest were linked together. Today a new goal seems possible: If enough habitat is restored, then someday the golden lion tamarins can be removed from the list of endangered species. ★

October 10:
CHURCHILL, MANITOBA

We came to the shore of Hudson Bay in Churchill, Manitoba, to learn about polar bears. The great white bears were recently added to the list of endangered species. The bears were listed as threatened. That means they aren't in critical danger yet, but they could be soon. We wondered why the bears might be in trouble.

To learn more, we drove across the tundra in a special vehicle for viewing polar bears. Soon we saw a mother walking with her two cubs. Then we saw a group of male bears.

Life on Ice

Polar bears don't normally live on land. Sea ice is the polar bears' habitat. On ice they live, breed, and hunt for seals. We wondered why the bears were not on the ice this late in autumn.

Every year the bears of Hudson Bay come to shore. The ice on the bay melts each summer. Polar bears cannot hunt in open water. So they come onto land and wait several months for the ice to freeze again. The bears are used to this. Their bodies have adapted to go without food.

They live off their body fat and become thinner. As winter approaches, the ice freezes again. Then the bears travel back onto Hudson Bay to hunt.

Problems for Polar Bears

The problem is that Hudson Bay is growing warmer. Many scientists believe greenhouse gases released from factories, buildings, and vehicles are causing climate change. These gases stay in the air and trap heat from the sun. Because Hudson Bay is warmer now, the sea ice melts sooner than it once did. The ice-free season lasts longer, which means polar bears are going longer without food. Polar bears are adapted to go without food, but there is a limit to how long they can wait. They need time to hunt and grow fat again.

GREENHOUSE GASES

The changing climate is a problem for people, animals, and plants all over the world. You can help by using less electricity. Making electricity releases greenhouse gases. Turn off lights, televisions, radios, and computers when you are not using them. Cars also produce greenhouse gases. When you can, walk or ride a bicycle instead of taking a car.

Polar bears need sea ice to survive.

The bears of Hudson Bay are growing thinner. Fewer bears live in the bay now. Scientists think these changes are caused by the shorter ice season. These changes may be the first signs that polar bears are in trouble.

Many scientists predict that Earth's atmosphere will keep getting warmer. If that happens, the ice-free time will keep growing longer. The problem is happening not just in Hudson Bay, but all over the Arctic. The polar bears may not be able to survive if there is not enough ice. They could someday be endangered. ★

For our last stop, we came to Blackwater National Wildlife Refuge in Maryland to learn about bald eagles. As we came into the park, we spotted eagles perched high in the trees. We watched the eagles from a distance so we wouldn't scare them away.

Eagles in Danger

Later we stopped at the park office where we talked with a park ranger. He explained that once it had seemed that bald eagles were headed for extinction in the lower 48 states. Many people hunted bald eagles. Some people believed that bald eagles carried off young calves and lambs from farms. In some places there was a reward for eagles caught. Hunters killed hundreds of thousands of eagles.

All this hunting was bad for the eagle population. Year after year, the number of bald eagles decreased. People eventually realized there weren't many eagles left. It appeared that the bald eagle would become extinct in the United States.

The bald eagle used to be endangered.

The U.S. government made the first law to protect the eagles in 1940. Hunting eagles was banned. Some people hoped this would be enough to help the species recover.

Then a new threat came. Pollution in the environment began making the eagles sick. One of the substances was

DDT, a pesticide. Farmers sprayed DDT on their crops to kill insects. The government sprayed DDT to kill mosquitoes. The pesticide washed into rivers and lakes. It ended up in fish, the eagles' food. DDT and other kinds of pollution were poisoning the birds.

Making a Comeback

The U.S. government passed a new law banning DDT in 1972. The eagles' health improved, and the population of eagles grew. People spotted eagles nesting in places where the birds hadn't been seen for years. In 2007, the U.S. government announced that the bird had recovered. It was taken off the endangered species list. Today the bald eagle is a great success story of how endangered animals can recover if people care enough to take action. ★

PROTECTING BALD EAGLES TODAY

The U.S. government continues to study the bald eagle and make sure it is safe. It is still illegal for people to harm bald eagles or tamper with their nests.

MISSION ACCOMPLISHED!

Congratulations! You have learned that many animals around the world are in trouble. You have learned that an endangered animal is one that is in danger of becoming extinct. You have learned that animals can become endangered when they are hunted too much or poisoned by pollution. They can become endangered when the places they live in are destroyed or broken into small patches. You've also learned how people have helped endangered animals. People have bred some animals such as the golden lion tamarin in zoos and reintroduced them into the wild. Governments have passed laws to prevent pollution and hunting from harming animal populations. People have worked to save and reconnect animal habitats. Congratulations on a great mission!

CONSIDER THIS

Consider other ways you might help save endangered animals. By asking yourself more questions about saving endangered animals, you might just start a mission of your own!

How can you help endangered animals?

★ How do adaptations help animals survive in their habitats?

★ Why do people want to save endangered animals?

★ What are some successful methods people have used to save endangered animals?

★ What can you do to help endangered animals?

GLOSSARY

atmosphere (AT-muhss-fihr) the air that surrounds
the planet

birthrate (BURTH-rayt) the number of babies born
each year

conservationist (kon-sur-VAY-shuhn-ist) a person who
works to save wild places, plants, and animals

greenhouse gases (GREEN-houss GASS-siz) gases that trap
heat in the atmosphere

habitat (HAB-uh-tat) the specific place where an animal
or plant lives

habitat fragmentation (HAB-uh-tat frag-men-TAY-shuhn)
the breaking up of habitat into separate areas

nature reserve (NAY-chur ri-SURV) land set aside for
wildlife

poacher (POHCH-ur) someone who hunts illegally

pollution (puh-LOO-shuhn) harmful substances released
into the air, soil, or water

population (pop-yuh-LAY-shuhn) the number of a
particular species living in one place

reintroduce (ree-in-truh-DOOS) to release captive
animals back into their habitats

LEARN MORE

BOOKS

Charman, Andrew. *I Wonder Why the Dodo Is Dead: and Other Questions About Extinct and Endangered Animals.* Boston: Kingfisher, 2007.

Mills, Andrea. *Animals Like Us: The World's Endangered Creatures Speak Out.* New York: DK Publishing, 2005.

WEB SITES

"Amazing Animals Family of Sites." National Geographic Kids.
http://kids.nationalgeographic.com/Animals
Learn about many different kinds of animals.

"Dealing with Endangered Species Game." San Diego Zoo.
http://www.sandiegozoo.org/kids/games/dwes.html
Play a card-matching game about endangered animals.

"Polar Bear Kids Zone." World Wildlife Fund.
http://www.panda.org/what_we_do/where_we_work/arctic/
area/species/polarbear/polar_bear/kids_zone/
Play games to learn more about saving polar bears and the Arctic.

CREATE A GREENHOUSE IN A JAR

You can learn how greenhouse gases work by creating a greenhouse in a jar. Sunlight passes through the glass walls of a jar. Inside the jar, the light changes to heat. Heat cannot pass through the glass. It stays trapped inside the jar, just as heat stays trapped in Earth's atmosphere. Lay two jars on their sides in a sunny spot, either outside or on a windowsill. Put a thermometer in each jar. Cover the top of one jar with a lid or plastic wrap. Leave the other jar open. After 15 minutes, compare the temperatures inside the two jars.

CREATE AN ANIMAL-FRIENDLY BACKYARD

Whether your outdoor space is big or small, you can make it friendly to animals. The National Wildlife Federation (NWF) shows you how to create a habitat for animals. You'll learn how to give animals what they need: food, water, and shelter. When your animal habitat is done, you can apply to make your garden a NWF Certified Wildlife Habitat. Follow the steps on the NWF Web site, http://www.nwf.org/gardenforwildlife/create.cfm.

30

INDEX

adapt, 4, 20-21

babies, 9-10, 13, 17, 19
bans, 13, 24-25
breeding, 16-17, 20

climate change, 21-22

eagles, 23-25
elephants, 9-11
extinct, 4, 6, 13, 16, 19, 23

food, 6, 8, 10, 11, 17, 19,
    20-21, 25
fragmented, 8, 16

greenhouse gases, 21

habitat loss, 6-8, 10, 16, 19,
    20-22
hunting, 12-13, 23-24

pandas, 6-8
poachers, 10-11
polar bears, 20-22
pollution, 24-25
population, 12-13, 15, 17, 23,
    25

recovery, 13, 15, 16, 19,
    24-25
reintroduction, 17, 19
reserve, 8, 9-11, 17, 19
rules, 15

study, 14-15, 20

tamarins, 16-19

war, 11
water, 8, 9-10, 20, 25
whales, 12-15

zoos, 16-19

ABOUT THE AUTHOR

Rebecca E. Hirsch, PhD, writes books about science and the environment for children. A former molecular biologist, she writes from her home in State College, Pennsylvania, where she lives with her husband and three children.

ABOUT THE CONSULTANTS

Mark Andersen is a wildlife ecologist at New Mexico State University. He teaches courses on population ecology, research methods in ecology and natural resources, and ecological risk assessment. He does research using computer simulations of ecological systems to help solve conservation and environmental problems.

Gail Saunders-Smith is a former classroom teacher and Reading Recovery teacher leader. Currently she teaches literacy courses at Youngstown State University in Ohio. Gail is the author of many books for children and three professional books for teachers.